Betty

First Published 2023
© text Nia Morais, 2023
© illustrations Anastasia Magloire, 2023

No part of this publication may be reproduced, stored in a retrieval system,
or transmitted, in any form, or by any means, electrical, mechanical, photocopying,
recording or otherwise without the prior permission of the publisher or a licence
permitting restricted copying.

ISBN 978-1-914303-32-6

Published by Llyfrau Broga Books, Whitchurch, Cardiff

www.broga.cymru

Betty

The Determined Life of Betty Campbell

Written by Nia Morais
Illustrated by Anastasia Magloire

Betty Campbell was born in 1934 in Tiger Bay, Cardiff. It was a busy place full of people from all over the world.

Lots of the people who lived in Tiger Bay had spent many weeks on a ship to get to Wales.

Betty's mother came from Cardiff and her father was a sailor from Jamaica. When she was eight he died at sea.

After this, times were hard for the family but their close community helped them so Betty didn't go without.

Little Betty loved school and decided that she wanted to be a teacher when she grew up. She worked hard to pass a difficult exam for a place in one of the city's best schools.

One day, Betty's headteacher asked what she'd like to do for a living.

When Betty said that she dreamt of being a teacher, the headteacher looked at her in shock. She told her that she could never be a teacher because of the colour of her skin.

This made Betty sad and angry but even more determined to succeed – no matter how difficult it might be.

She studied hard and was often top of her class.

Soon after leaving school Betty fell in love with a boy from Jamaica called Rupert.

They got married and had children, and soon all of Betty's time was spent looking after her happy family.

When her children were still young Betty heard that a local teaching college was accepting women for the first time.

She had never forgotten her dream of being a teacher and started as one of the first-ever female students on the course.

Betty's dream came true. She was delighted to get a job as headteacher of Mount Stuart Primary, a new school in the old docklands of Cardiff where she'd grown up.

Some thought the docks were a dangerous place but Betty knew that it was a special community, full of history and love.

Betty was the first Black headteacher in Wales.

She was determined to teach the children of the docks their history and the history of Black people all over the world.

With Betty as leader the school was very successful and became famous.

Lots of people came from all over the world to visit Betty Campbell's inspiring school.

Because the history of Black people was so important to her Betty helped to inspire UK Black History Month, to celebrate the successes and contribution of Black people in Wales and beyond.

SHIRLEY BASSEY

BILLY BOSTON

RICHARD PARKS

KIZZY CRAWFORD

Betty continued to support the Docklands throughout her life, even after retiring.

She made sure that everyone was looked after and that the children could get to school safely.

Betty loved her community and everyone in the Docklands knew her and was very proud of her.

In 2017 Betty was chosen to be the subject of the first statue of a woman erected in Wales. Today her statue stands in Cardiff's central square.

Betty Campbell made a name for herself in Welsh history. But, for her, the most important thing was teaching people that everybody is equal. Everyone should be able to celebrate their skin colour and have an equal opportunity to succeed in life.

Read about more Welsh Wonders

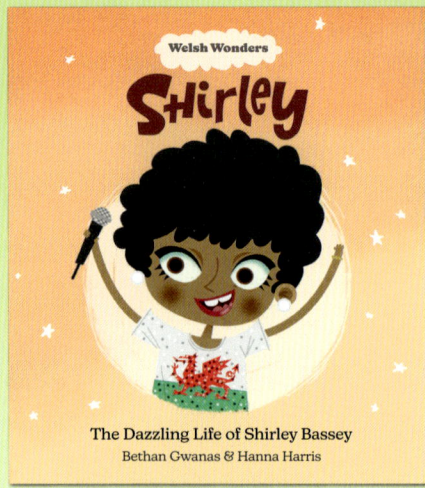

Shirley Bassey
The girl from Tiger Bay whose voice became famous around the world.

Cranogwen
Sarah Jane Rees was a sea captain, prize-winning poet, publisher, and inspiration!

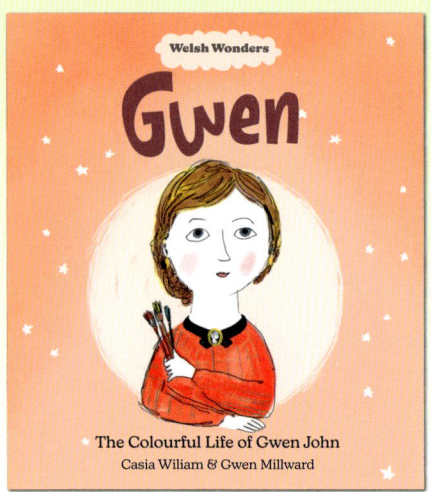  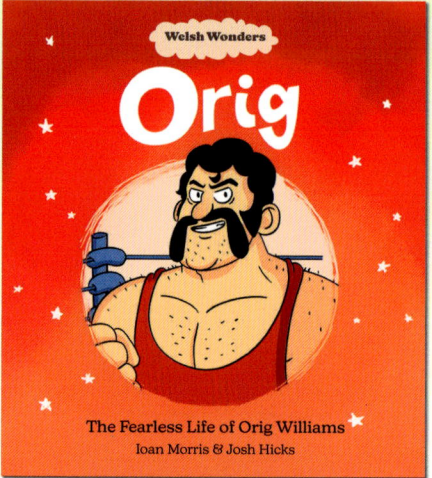

Gwen John
A shy but determined girl who loved to paint and followed her dream of being a famous artist.

Orig Williams
The tough-guy wrestler with a heart of gold, known around the world as El Bandito!

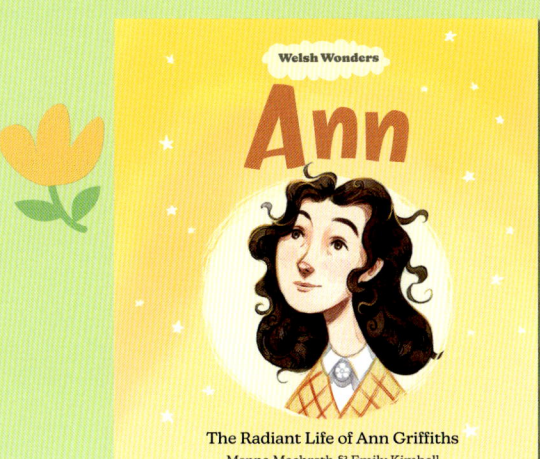

Ann Griffiths
The sensitive poet whose spiritual songs inspired millions.

Aneurin Bevan
Inspirational politician who founded the NHS and changed a nation.

Laura Ashley
Fashion designer who built a business empire from her home in mid Wales.

Alfred Russel Wallace
The adventurous naturalist who travelled the world and made incredible discoveries.

Find out more about other inspiring Welsh lives – from artists and scientists to people who challenged the way things were and overcame difficulties to achieve their dreams.